GOD WOOS

Copyright Ralph Wright O.S.B. © 2021. All rights reserved.

No part of this book may be used or reproduced by any means, graphic, electronic, or mechanical, including photocopying, recording, taping or by any information storage retrieval system without the written permission of the publisher.

Published by Mater Media
St. Louis, Missouri
www.matermedia.org

Cover and Interior Design: Trese Gloriod

Printed in the USA.

ISBN: 978-1-7365190-4-2

FAVORITE POEMS OF
A MONK-PRIEST
1970 - 2020

GOD WOOS

By
Ralph Wright O.S.B.

MATER MEDIA

CONTENTS

Orchid	1
A Cloud Watcher	2
Cheery Thought On A Rainy Morning	4
When God Made You	5
The Child In The Womb	6
Hubble And DNA	8
Unquenchable Love	11
Obsession	12
Ground For Joy	13
My God, My God…	14
Jesus	16
From All Eternity	17
Although Dust	18
Conceive	19
Every Christian Mother	21
The Mist Lifts	22
If You Are Made	23
The Astronomical	24
The Gospel Is	25
When The Last River	26
The Conjugal Act	28
A Spouse's Prayer	29
Let Your Face Shine On Us	30
Great Calm	31

Birthday Utterance	32
God Has An Exclusive	34
Cosmogony	35
Annunciation	36
Becoming Man	37
Message From Mary	38
Leaf Fall	39
God Woos	41
Fall Beauty	42
The Total Mighty	43
The Rage Of Hatred	44
Discrimination	46
In War	48
How Must It Be For God	49
O Extravagant	50
Unsurprised By Darkness	52
Seamless	54
Glory	56
My Peace	57
God Made Man Free	58
Learn From Me	60
The Highpriestly Prayer	61
The Regal Dark Mysterious Cross	62
Sing Of One Who Walks Beside Us	64
Beyond The Rubble	65
Apologia	67

Unique	68
Welcome	70
Arrival	71
Having Survived	72
Leaves	73
Snow	74
Motherhood	75
St. Louis Freezing Rain, Postlude	76
Why War	78
If God	79
A Leafwatcher	80
Life Is Simpler Towards Evening	82
Corpus Christi	84
Pivotal	85
Leaves Of Water	86
The Tree	87
Ants	88
Messiah	90
The Cosmic Incarnation	93
Infinite Patience	94
Death	96
Deus Caritas Est	98

ORCHID

The Parthenon,
the Taj Mahal,
Saint Peter's Rome
—Man's finest hour—
all stammer and are mute before
the architecture of a flower.

A CLOUD WATCHER

I have become
a watcher of clouds
in Wyoming
where the sky
is God's own canvas.
He begins with a wash of white
upon the purest blue
as our horses
climb rugged trails
along the river
and up, up,
towards the rough
rock disorder
of the mountains.

By noon they are billowing
out like pure white foam
soaring above the cresting
silhouettes of pines
that sway like sentinels
and watch the winding water
creeping far below.

Sometimes they muster ranks
and with a splash of darkness
mutate with sudden grandeur
into storms
lashing the rocks and water
with their lightning.
They drench us with the coolness
of their rain
achieving new fragrances
of pine and scrub
and blended herbal bushes.
But dusk is kept
unsparingly
for glory
as the Artist's brush
selects the radiance of fire
from his palette
to paint in orange,
gold, and crimson blood
a final fanfare
of tremendous passion
as day succumbs to night.

CHEERY THOUGHT ON A RAINY MORNING

if You didn't need to
but only made me
because You loved me
what an unbelievably
marvelous being
I must be
designed
by the One Lover
only to be
perfectly beloved

WHEN GOD MADE YOU

When
God
made
you
there
was
silence
in
heaven
for
five
minutes.
Then
God
said:
"How come I never thought of that before?"

THE CHILD IN THE WOMB

How can one clarify
the nonchalant barbarity
of killing one's own children

—miscarriage
may be a way.

When a new couple
conceives
their first child

the hopes and the longings
multiply
with the speculation
will it be
a boy or a girl?

Names are already
talked about
and suggested.
It is already a person.
Premature
death
is a sadness
alleviated
only by the hope
of another child.

The very thought
of provoking
a miscarriage
is unthinkable.

But in our culture
the distance to travel
for the procedure
defines
the morality
of termination.

HUBBLE AND DNA

Hubble
shows—
or reminds us
of the age
of the universe.

The eons of light-years
it took
to form the cosmos
and eons later
to form the earth.

How long did it take
before the earth
was ready
to receive the Lord
in Bethlehem?

How long was the cosmos
waiting
for each conceptus
each 'you'
and each 'me'?

And if we were
terminated
how great
the sadness would be.

Never again
would that sperm
and that ovum
unite
to be this person.

Each termination
prevents this
conceptus
from ever inhabiting
this universe.

UNQUENCHABLE LOVE

if I could only see you, Lord,
as you are
a wild Lover
intent on loving
absolutely
each beloved—
unless prevented
by the wild horses of an untamed
savage will—
I would know the desire
in your heart
and would beg
on my knees
each day
the grace
to tame
my savagery
and so
unbar the door
and let my Beloved
enter
the quiet stable of a bridled heart.

OBSESSION

people say
why are Catholics
so obsessed
by sex

but

only through sex
do we work
directly
with God

pro-creating
new members
for his family

each person
someone new
destined
by his love
one day
to share God's life

GROUND FOR JOY

My past lies
in the merciful hands of God

my future
in His wise love

the present moment
in which I live
is of no duration

how then may fear win
mastery over my joy?

MY GOD, MY GOD...

The killing of tiny people
in the womb
has become
more horrific
—like crucifixion—
as we have
explored the process.

The way in which
each part of the body
becomes
through DNA
a reflection
of the parent
makes dismemberment
the tearing apart
more gross
or more barbaric.

We must
find required alternatives
to this
inhumanity.

We must
present
to the mother
ways to bring
her child to birth
that respect
the Creator's stunning
and
unique majesty
in the union of sperm and ovum
that is a person.

And His longing that this child
one day
— through Jesus —
might share
his eternal life.

JESUS

Jesus
in the womb
for me
let me know
the love I see

Jesus
on the cross
for me
let me know
the love I see

Jesus
in the host
for me
let me know
the love I see

FROM ALL ETERNITY

From all eternity
You made me
as if to be
your only spouse
in time
may I choose You
to be mine

ALTHOUGH DUST

Although dust
I am loved
by the one
eternal
Son of the Father
just as intensely
as this same Father
loves his one
eternal Son

O mystery
O majesty
O wonder
that what we
in our wildest dreams
could not conceive
has been
by God's own Word
quietly revealed.

CONCEIVE

to bring
and to have brought
into being
through God

one called
to live forever
intimately
with God

what a stunning
mind-scalding
thing to do
and to have done

could anything
conceivably
be greater —
none.

EVERY CHRISTIAN MOTHER

every Christian mother
watches God
in her first-born
come
into the world
and with amazed
shocked
wonder
knows that the mystery
of Love
eluding
the handling of the mind
resembles more
twin squirrels
chasing each other
on either side
of a tree
than crashes of thunder
waking us at midnight
to Wagnerian lightning

THE MIST LIFTS

the mist lifts

for a moment

over the why of creation

as I see

God

making each person

with the identical

wonder and joy

of making

Jesus

IF YOU ARE MADE

If you are made
Man
by God
to share his life
then nothing
They may say
or do
can ever reduce
the barely finite
grandeur
of your being.

THE ASTRONOMICAL

The
astronomical
nature
of
Your
love
for
me
is
revealed
by
my
repentance
unbar
the
doors
and
let
the
dawn
light
blaze
in
!

THE GOSPEL IS

The
Gospel
is
that
we
are
each
unique

uniquely
made
uniquely
loved
uniquely
died for.

WHEN THE LAST RIVER

When the last river has let its waters
meet the sea,
when the last cloud has let its rain
touch the waves,
when the last breeze has brought coolness
to the face of man
and the last sun has bowed its head
behind the mountains,
I will reach down and raise you up,
says the Lord,
to be with me, your brother,
for ever.

THE CONJUGAL ACT

An act between
A husband and wife
Expressing love
And open to life.

A SPOUSE'S PRAYER

I am made free
in the image of God
that my love may be total
for you and my God

may our love be faithful
through the grace of our God
may it also be fruitful
in people of God.

LET YOUR FACE SHINE ON US

You came
In Mary's womb
That we might see
Your face.

"To see me, Philip,
is to see the Father."

We
Choose
To terminate
Our children
before they might see
even their mother's
face.

And in her
See You,
O Jesus.

GREAT CALM

I am filled with joy
that God loves you
with great competence
for my love
is infinite
in clumsiness
when I wound
He heals
when I damage
He restores
and you are always
in his hands
O great calm
O mighty God
O quiet joy.

BIRTHDAY UTTERANCE

I have great joy
in knowing that you
have been
born
into the world
because
having been breathed
by God
into existence
you will never
be able
— like a bubble —
to pop
suddenly
back into nothingness

GOD HAS AN EXCLUSIVE

God
has
an
exclusive
love
for
each
person
He
creates.

COSMOGONY

It is the moment of new life
The moment of conception
That is the most sacred
Most holy
Most marvelous
Cosmic event.

Therefore
From that moment
Each
Human life
Must be revered
And protected
Not from the first heartbeat.

ANNUNCIATION

The acute load of a great joy
needles my heart
and seethes within the tissues of my brain—
the thought that this the face of man became,
on some brief long-forgotten day,
the face of God — and will remain
O may this joy beneath life's puzzling goad
each day explode!

BECOMING MAN

The humble moment
of total fusion
in darkness
and silence
seen by no one
heard by no one
felt by no one
a greater detonation
than any nuclear fission
and for a long while yet
no one will know it has happened.

MESSAGE FROM MARY

Jesus
Asked me
To tell you
"I'm
Glad
That you didn't
Eliminate
Me."

LEAF FALL

I was not watching but I heard
a leaf fall off an indoor plant just now
and hit the carpet in the perfect stillness —
as it fell it touched another leaf
and so I heard its fall —
there was no kind of wind or other force
to cause this brief event, it seems it fell
simply because it had been growing
silently old long enough
to earn this parting —
it may be at least a week or even a month
before another leaf from the same plant
merits this moment.
So what a simple grace and gift it was,
and quite uncalled for,
to be there at this instant not to watch
- as one might watch a lift-off towards the moon -
but, as befits its call to be discreet,
only to hear the falling of this leaf.

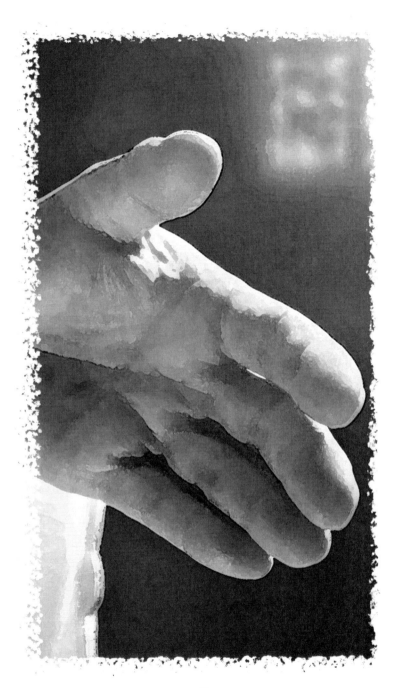

GOD WOOS

God woos
Our Love
He can't
Coerce

At first the cave
The manger bed
Then back to Joseph's
Doors and chairs

He makes
The wine at Cana
Then back home
To chairs and tables
Woodwork
Good woodwork

And while he works
God woos
Love works
It can't coerce.

FALL BEAUTY

reflected in the window of the door
aslant against the midnight purple wall
the leaves outside are dancing in the wind
in yellow amber green and sudden gold

so great an exhibition of His work
in casual excess
is always hard to find
and yet

the claim is limited
that one brief leaf may have on our concern
while God
to whom you'd think we would appear as leaves
has proved the hold we have upon his heart
as limited as nails into trees.

THE TOTAL MIGHTY

The
Total mighty
Omni-loving God
With infinite respect
For that continent of mystery
Freedom-wielding
Man
Hides
Within a child
Omnipotence
Lest anything but love
Should bring
Our watching hearts
to fall in love with him.

THE RAGE OF HATRED

Christmas 1914
at the Front
German and British
soldiers
arranged a truce.

They sang carols
exchanged cigars
brandy
and plum pudding.
They played soccer
in No Man's Land.

The generals
back at HQ,
we're told,
were furious.

Nobody wants
to kill his brother
once he knows him
as a person.

The rage
and folly
of hatred
has to be stoked
by calumny,
ignorance
and lies.

We must not think
of his wife
at home
or of his children
hoping for his return.

We have to demonize
our enemy
at the Front
to nurture
our hatred,
if we are
to bayonet him
or blow him away,
Before he has finished
his plum pudding,
drunk our brandy,
or smoked right through
one of our cigars.

DISCRIMINATION

How come I trust,
selectively,
the laws that science finds
and builds upon?

I trust that the brakes in my Ford Focus,
especially at rush hour,
will prevent collision.
I trust the planes that hold me
in the sky
will bring me safely down.

I trust the anesthetist,
who puts me out for surgery,
will bring me back.

I trust the wheat seed cast into the field
will bring me bread
for my table.

I trust the internet will send my greeting
to you in Australia
at the speed of light.

I trust the hens will bring me
scrambled eggs
for tomorrow's breakfast.

I trust both scientific demonstrated wisdom
and my own (and your)
common sense.

And yet in face of both of these
I withhold my conviction
That every human being
begins at conception.

IN WAR

In war
people without hate
learn to kill
people without hate
this is why
it is
totally obscene

HOW MUST IT BE FOR GOD

How must it be for God,
who hides beneath a Calvary of pain
the massive love he has for each of us,
to know with absolute precision
the mammoth nature of our unconcern,
the cold of our indifference?

Yet he is so afraid of drawing love
for less than kosher motives that he hides
and chooses that his Son should not be seen
except within the guise of one despised;
and that his gentle love should stay unknown
except by those whose almost foolish trust
leads them to tread the path that he once trod
and know, as one ignored and mocked by men,
the wonder of the love beyond the pain.

O EXTRAVAGANT

O extravagant
patient God
taking billions
of years to cool
molten light
till life might ripen
into consciousness
competent for your godhead

O unknown
humble God
choosing to come
without glamor
among the dung
of steaming cattle
and so become
"the eldest of many brothers."

O meticulous
lowly God
choosing to go
without magnificence
nailed between
your brother thieves
proving with un-
ambiguous deeds
how pure the God
who so conceives.

UNSURPRISED BY DARKNESS

If God's own Son
had to brink despair
dying in the darkness
of noonday night

why should I
know a tranquil passage
from finite groping
to infinite Light?

Why am I shocked
by the daily trauma
woven into
the heart of flesh;

the rending anger
perdures from the womb
till the hands are folded
in the calm of death.

See the stars
and ponder the Word
in whom each galaxy
finds its being;

then watch the one
whose humble coming
respects the measure
of our seeing.

For "who can live
with a blazing fire?"
O mercifully mercifully
hidden God

coming as breeze
coming as bread
coming through the grape
our feet have trod.

SEAMLESS

Stretched between tall grass in the dawn light
the cobweb shimmers—
rainbows,
magic innocence,
routine evil.

The fighters with folded wings
stand at parade as the carrier moves
through Mediterranean blue,
inspected annually by the Queen
an admiral at each elbow.

Even the spider moves like a priest
towards his breakfast sacrifice,
but how does the fly feel
caught on the wire
before and after the jaws?

I sat at the back of the church.
Under the dome a spider hung
caught like a copter in the sun.
A tiny lump of gold it soared and plunged,
soared and plunged.
A trapeze artist high in the Big Top.
A secretary typing a routine letter
in total silence.
A seamstress mending a torn and seamless robe.

GLORY

I have felt
the crucifixion
of the Word
upon the sidewalk
after the heavy rain
and the sound
was like one screaming
"I am a man
and no worm!"
but in the darkness
my foot
ignored
his glory.

MY PEACE

I give peace
my peace
a deepness and a calm that keeps
the high waves of grief or pain,
of growing distance or indifference
from shattering your frail faith.

Peace I give
my peace
forged each day upon the anvil of
your crucified and yet undying
pride.

Peace
my peace
the peace that keeps depression from despair
that finds within the darkest woods
moments of sunlight where the leaves
beam slow smoke in the autumn air.
Keeping the hope that in a while
all that here is only seen
savored shared or understood
when it is past
always will be yours
within my kingdom.

GOD MADE MAN FREE

God made man free
To get things wrong
He made the atom
We the bomb.

LEARN FROM ME

The grain pounded
to powder
mixed with water
rolled and baked
to become
ordinary bread

The grapes harvested
trodden
strained
and kept to become
in time
ordinary wine

The Tree of Agony
the Empty Tomb
breakfast on the shore
"If you love me,
Simon Peter,
feed my lambs."

Intimacy with God
no ordinary food

THE HIGHPRIESTLY PRAYER

O Father, it is my desire
That those You gave to me
Should be with me that where I am
My friends may also be.
To them I have revealed your love,
Your truth, your life, your way;
And now a word abides in them
Which shall not pass away.

The glory that You gave to me,
To them I now have given;
That so they may be one on earth
As we are one in heaven.
Do not, O Father, take them from
The world your hands have made;
But keep them from the Evil one,
From all that is depraved.

And teach them how to give their lives
That new life may abound.
In giving all they find our love
And in that love are found.
O Father, it is my desire
That all may live as one,
With You in me and I in them
So shall your Kingdom come.

THE REGAL DARK MYSTERIOUS CROSS

The regal dark mysterious cross
In song is lifted high,
The wood on which our God was raised
As Man against the sky.

Upon this wood his body bore
The nails, the taunts, the spear,
Till water flowed with blood to wash
The whole world free of fear.

At last the song that David sung
Is heard and understood:
"Before the nations God as King
Reigns from his throne of wood."

This wood now spread with purple wears
The pageantry of kings;
Of chosen stock it dares to hold
On high his tortured limbs.

O blessed Tree, upon whose arms
The world's own ransom hung;
His body pays our debt and life
From Satan's grasp is wrung.

O sacred Cross, our steadfast hope
In this our Passiontide,
Through you the Son obtained for all
Forgiveness as he died.

May every living creature praise
Our God both one and three,
Who rules in everlasting peace
All whom his cross makes free.

SING OF ONE WHO WALKS BESIDE US

Sing of one who walks beside us
And this day is living still,
One who now is closer to us
Than the thoughts our hearts distill,
One who once upon a hilltop
Raised against the power of sin,
Died in love as his own creatures
Crucified their God and King.

Strangers we have walked beside him
The long journey of the day,
And have told him of the darkness
That has swept our hope away.
He has offered words of comfort,
Words of energy and light,
And our hearts have blazed within us
As he saved us from the night.

Stay with us, dear Lord, and raise us,
Once again the night is near.
Dine with us and share your wisdom.
Free our hearts from every fear.
In the calm of each new evening,
In the freshness of each dawn,
If you hold us fast in friendship
We will never be alone.

BEYOND THE RUBBLE

40,000 citizens,
Multiples of one,
Die
As the first
Bomb explodes.

100,000
Live
As unconditional
Surrender
Is slowly declared.

War ends
And silence returns.

Should we ban
The bomb
Or build
A larger one?

Peace
Out of fear
Is still peace.

And I will show you fear
In a handful of dust.

APOLOGIA

you have explained
to me
born blind
the smile
on
Mona Lisa

and I know it
as well
as a man
born deaf
knows

the last notes
of the taps bugle
fading
into silence

UNIQUE

unique
is the clue
to God's creation

unique
is the clue
to our redemption

three hours
of agony
upon the cross

chosen
by the One
in whom
all
was created

to bring
to union
with him

each single
person
whom he created

from nothing
only for love

to be
with him
eternally
in being

WELCOME

Welcome
to this one great
champagne
dancing
party of being
and be
always
alive and utterly
grateful to Him
who
simply freely spontaneously
needlessly and
eternally
utters.

ARRIVAL

as a new

fiancé

waiting

at the airport

beyond 'security'

for the arrival

of the beloved

so You

await the

coming

of each one of us

into eternity

HAVING SURVIVED

Having survived
life in the womb
which so many do not
these days
(Chicago alone terminates 21000 each year)
and having lived
some 80 Christmases,
I know what it's like
to breathe the scent
of the despised honeysuckle
or of the admired first daffodil
and to be
now
but one breath away
from eternity.

LEAVES

leaves

have become

—like Monet's lilypads—

part of my paradise

SNOW

The paratroopers of the winter sky
locust the earth
some come compelled
driven by gusts towards the harmless ground
that fights back green against them
some drift with counterfeit contentment
veterans of the ebb and flow of years
hitting the turf and welcoming
the sun's annihilation
some dance and let the wind
play kindly with them
absorbing to the full
the ecstasy of space
with ballerina grace they move
while the sun hides
the sky is grey
and silence is their music.

MOTHERHOOD

I thank you, Father,
For you have given me
Someone whose heart
Will live for ever.
Someone to love me
And be loved by me;
Someone to know me
And know my name.

His father loved me
And so began
His journey from me
Within your hand.
May our love blossom
That we may raise
New names to know You
And give you praise.

You gave your life once
That we might know you.
You chose the pain
To conquer our sin.
And now with the wonder
That Love makes known
New flames are kindled
To bless your name.

ST. LOUIS FREEZING RAIN, POSTLUDE

The icicles are trees this morning
in crystal wonderlands that burst the heart
all the Fabergés of every art
since cave men sketched their bison on the walls
are children building castles on the sand
compared to these —
twigs and limbs with every hang of ice
poise paradise in filaments of light
splintered through a million perfect prisms
throwing a circuit-breaker in our heads
lest overload should burn away the mind
and leave us foolish

and yet You chose in wisdom to forego
this icescape ecstasy when You came
to live a lifetime here so long ago
if You had come to Palestine today
You could yourself have seen with your own eyes
this sparkle kingdom that was gone by noon
with your own eyes You could yourself have seen
and then been
back at the Beautiful Gate for evening prayer
by special Concorde via Tel Aviv
to hear the bombs go off and drink the wine
and see the sun go down and yet You chose
to see it all through mine.

WHY WAR

Distance gives the Men of War their power,
Kept to keep me capable of hate.
I cannot hate the one I do not know
And lest I know
They keep between us space.

Numbers may be bombed at will,
Erased from charts and left in tombs.
But men are made of love in wombs
And persons are too close to kill.

Idealogians smile and wash their hands,
They calmly state the final terms for peace.
If they would let me know you as a man,
It would suffice.

IF GOD

if God

had been

indifferent

to you

He'd

have

made

someone

else

A LEAFWATCHER

I have far too much joy
in watching the leaves
falling

for a whole minute
none fall
and then

four
leaves
fall
in different
demonstrations
of
delight
like divers
in the Olympics

one pirouettes
an almost
corkscrew motion
straight down

another
like a stunt parachutist
uses the wind
for
guidance

another
like a marine
waits till when he thinks
that no one
is watching
then
slips silently down
to avoid detection

another
drops nonchalantly down
after a long season
of
clinging

when they reach the ground
beneath my window
all
settle comfortably down

embarking on
the dull business
of
becoming
loam

LIFE IS SIMPLER TOWARDS EVENING

life is simpler towards evening
shadows longer quieter
and more complete
things are calm

we no longer throttle speech
from mystery
but having lived through long years
respect silence

we no longer audit God's accounts
with the same agony
but knowing him more deeply know that he
is good for loving

now vision comes
only in lightning
leaving us blinder than before
but more aware
that change remains our permanent despair

pulled by a current out of our control
we live in a growing past
the myth of happiness stains our empty glass
time corks the joy of every swift delight
but moments test the passing wine
and find in it a tang of the eternal

CORPUS CHRISTI

Man holds
within his hand
the one who holds
within his hand
the universe —
cup your hand in awe, O man,
and pray
that He who comes so humbly
unto you
as food
may make you worthy of himself
eternally
as God.

PIVOTAL

I stand

and watch

the universe

spin past me

like a carousel

a merry-go-round

with me

at the center

winding the wheel

or keeping the button pressed

all six of us

round the altar

hold the wafer

a little above

our hand

"This is the Lamb of God…"

what kind of God

to let his creatures

hold him thus

while the universe

goes flying by.

LEAVES OF WATER

I wonder did
God think of leaves
falling from
the autumn trees

before he thought
of flakes of snow
leaves of water
drifting so

gently in
December's breeze
they might have been
October's leaves.

THE TREE

the tree
exploded out of
winter silence
throwing shooting
stars of blossom
into the lake
where the sun
burnt
the evening away
and left no ashes

ANTS

in my wash basin
3 ½ periods move

I crush them
with my thumb

how amazing
that beings
this small
should know such movement

later I find
they move in armies
millions strong
and quite uncountable

how much thought
move or stay
rockstill
is in each tiny being

with hubble showing
the myriads out there
of time and cosmic
space
I wonder stunned
at each morning ant
moving or being still
on my desert enamel

MESSIAH

anoint the wounds
of my spirit
with the balm
of forgiveness
pour the oil
of your calm
on the waters
of my heart

take the squeal
of frustration
from the wheels
of my passion
that the power
of your tenderness
may smooth
the way I love

that the tedium
of giving
in the risk
of surrender
and the reaching
out naked
to a world
that must wound

may be kindled
fresh daily
to a blaze
of compassion
that the grain
may fall gladly
to burst in the ground
- and the harvest abound

THE COSMIC INCARNATION

The Cosmos keeps on moving
At lightspeed into space,
To measure time is useless
We move at God's own pace.

Our tiny earth a splinter
Struck from a star that died,
Provides when cooled to darkness
A place where life might thrive.

In years beyond all reckoning
Try millions to be sure
God made a being able
To love him or say "No"!

The "No" that Adam gave him
As Eve stood by his side,
Destroyed the "Yes" God longed for
And tore the cosmos wide.

But God whose love is perfect
Chose not to doom our race
But came as man to love us
And died to teach us "Yes."

INFINITE PATIENCE

God lets
his Son
be stretched
against
the earth
and nailed
to the wood
of the world

Behold
the mystery
of infinite
patience
that
God
should create
a being
able
to see

and love

or blindly

hate

then patiently

wait

and not

stop

the entire

show

when an innocent

child

weeps in the

night

or his Son

is stretched

against

the world

and brutally

nailed

DEATH

Father, I see You
running towards me
with open arms
as I crawl
through the narrow
passage of death.
I see You fling
your arms around me
as I stammer
"I am not worthy
to be called your son
treat me
as one of
your hired servants."

I hear You
call for the ring,
the sandals
the banquet.
And I hear You
cry out:
"Rejoice, rejoice,
you angels in heaven
for my son was lost
and is found.
My son was far
and has been brought near."
And the heavens
are filled
with rejoicing.

DEUS CARITAS EST

Jesus
Is
Head over heels
In love
With
Everyone
He died for.